I0188401

# Majical Love

## A Modern & Ancient Tale

*offered by*

*Gaia Waxman & Behnam Nouri*

Copyright © 2019 by Gaia Waxman and Behnam Nouri
All rights reserved.

Kiyan Publishing
1547 Palos Verdes Mall #234
Walnut Creek, CA. 94597

First Printing, 2019

Printed in the United States of America

Library of Congress Control Number: 2019901071
https://lccn.loc.gov/2019901071

ISBN 978-1-7336045-1-2

# Contents

# Artwork

# Introduction

The pursuit of romance,
with few notable exceptions,
is a relatively new development
in human evolution.

This may be surprising news ~
however, the romanticizing of
love first became popular in
the royal courts during
medieval times.

*Rather than describing a liaison laced with sexual attraction, the phrase "courtly love" conveyed a knight's devotion to honor and protect his Lord's lady.*

*In addition to physical protection of lords and ladies, training for knighthood included ethical conduct, respect for women, assistance for those in need, personal freedom, and self-realization.*

*Lofty ideals for the era!*

*Romanicus, which means
"of the Roman style" is said to be
the origin of the word "romance."*

*Research suggests that in the
late 1100s, Roman knights
retiring from duty sought out
a peaceful, luxurious locale
in southern France.*

*In their newly formed
retirement community, the
knights' training to cherish
the ladies they served continued
to deepen and develop.*

*Out of this emerging gallantry,*
*a new type of relational charm*
*arose between the sexes ~ now*
*with sensuality added to the mix.*

*The aristocracy of the time*
*became enamored with*
*the knights' pomp and*
*pageantry, and soon adopted*
*their chivalrous virtues ~*
*gentlemanly grace and courtesy*
*among them.*

*As a result of this evolution*
*in etiquette and gender*
*relations, more value was*
*afforded women.*

*Apparently early on, a romance signified an exciting, and well-rounded life.*

*It seems the recounting of our knights' tales led simultaneously to the advent of romantic love and the creation of the "novel" ~ dramatic accounts of human adventures in story form.*

*According to historians,
the meaning of the word "lovers"
in the Middle Ages referred to
psychological and emotional
intimacy, rather than today's
sexual connotation.*

*It was not until the late 17th
century that physical passion
was included as a further
refinement of courtly love ~
culminating into our current
concept of romance.*

*In ancient times, Greek philosopher, Aristotle, recognized an evolved love two people can attain, which he termed, "one soul and two bodies."*

*This love surpasses sexual desire, and offers a spiritual experience for the lovers.*

*Of course, we occasionally have heard tales of transcendent relationships occurring prior to this time.*

*However, the compelling ideal that every person can and should find a soul mate is a modern mental construct.*

*As humans evolve, so will our concept and practice of romantic love!*

*The following tale is a true story about two lovers who were gifted a metaphysical romance ~ surrendering to each other, their destiny, and unconditional love.*

*So watch for the bits and pieces that may be valuable to you!*

## First Encounter

Once upon a time, toward the
end of the twentieth century,
there lived, a handsome Persian
prince in San Ramon, California
~ of all places!

Although he was beautiful to
look at ~ held a degree in
engineering ~ was a masterful
watercolorist ~ pursued
a spiritual path ~ and was raised
in a loving family ~ he was a sad
and lonely fellow.

*It had been a year and a half since the end of a twelve-year relationship, and he was just beginning to be emotionally available for another affair of the heart.*

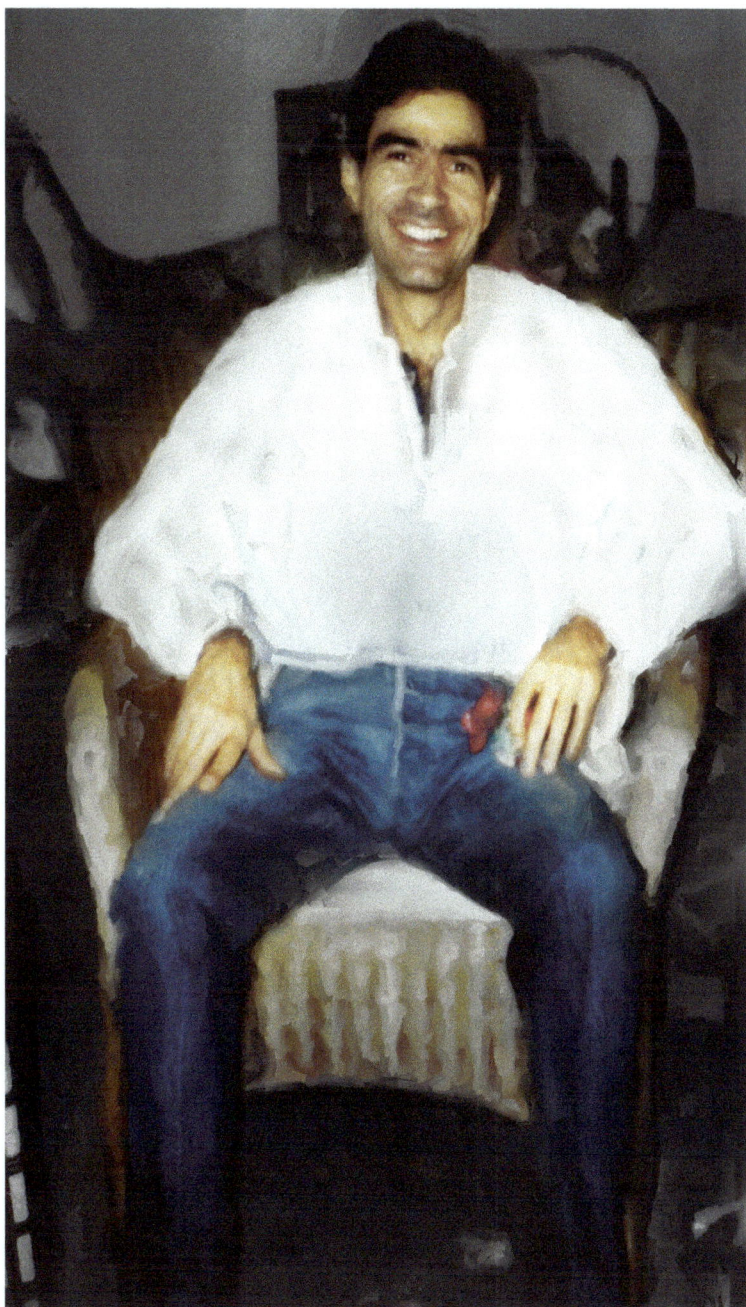

*One day as the prince was swimming in the pool at his apartment complex ~ a lovely lady came upon the scene.*

*He had never seen her there before and told her so.*

*She agreed she had not been to the pool much that summer ~ she'd been concentrating on course work for graduate school.*

*They exchanged identifying information such as spiritual interests, hobbies, and career choices.*

*But the lady was not about to give him any more information, especially her address.  As handsome and charming as he was, surely he was a player!*

*Moreover, she was departing the next day to spend a month visiting her family in New York ~ leaving her beautiful 23-year old daughter alone in their apartment.*

*As they finished their visit,*
*the handsome prince kissed*
*the lovely lady's hand*
*and told her the numbers of*
*his residence.*

*He then invited her to stop by*
*his humble abode*
*~ a cute one bedroom flat ~*
*so that they could continue their*
*conversation.*

When the lovely lady returned to her home, the beautiful daughter asked how the encounter had gone.

In fact, it had been her daughter who had seen the prince many times at the pool throughout that summer.

He was clearly stunning and peaceful ~ seemingly a great fit for the lovely lady.

Each time the handsome prince appeared poolside, the beautiful daughter would encourage her mother to go see him.

And always the lady answered she was too busy with her schoolwork to get involved with flirtations.

However, on this fateful day, the daughter left the pool, and quickly returned to the apartment ~ urging her mother once again.

The lovely lady agreed.

*Classes were finished for the semester, and she saw an opportunity to practice material presented in a Psychology of Spirituality course.*

*She had been introduced to the art of tantra ~ facing fears, inviting intimacy, and delving deeply into material form on a path to enlightenment.*

*So truth be told, the lady had gone to the pool expressly to meet this prince!*

*The beautiful daughter inquired whether her mother had mentioned that she would be gone for the coming month.*

*"No I didn't," said the lady. "If something is supposed to happen between us, he will be here when I get back."*

*While in New York, the lady noticed the prince frequently entered her thoughts.*

*She was feeling very attracted to him on many levels.*

After her return, she decided to
face her fears once more,
and see what might develop
with the Persian gentleman.

So one balmy evening the
lovely lady knocked on
the prince's door to invite him
on her nightly walk.

He was as charming and
handsome as she had
remembered.

Ladies were taught to be wary
of such men ~ and she was.

*The walk was going very well ~ lots of interesting conversation and animal magnetism.*

*Then the prince kissed the lady on the cheek.  This behavior startled the lady.*

*Alas, the prince could have only one thing in mind, and he was moving very quickly!*

*Unfortunately, she had no experience with Persian princes, and mistook his charming ways for shallow intentions.*

Yet the lady was still intrigued
with this handsome man ~ hence
she determined to move forward
slowly.

At walk's end, the prince invited
the lovely lady to his dwelling for
dinner the next night.

So much, so soon
~ but a man who cooks ~
this must be
investigated further!

The lady accepted the charming
prince's invitation.

However, instead of the usual
bottle of wine, she brought
the handsome prince
a flowering plant.

No imbibing for her this evening
~ she would need to keep her
wits about her.

Amazingly, the prince had
prepared a divine meal for them.
The lady was very impressed,
and happily dined ~ as she
usually did!

Years later, the prince revealed
how on that first
evening together, the lovely lady
appeared to him as a most
delicious peach ~ richly sweet
and juicy!

The lady was also very taken
with the handsome prince.

Great joy arose within her as
they chatted into the night about
a variety of mutual interests ~
music, art, travel, and spiritual
awakening.

*She had never seen a more handsome man with such wonderful balance: masculine/feminine ~ left brain/right brain ~ engineer/artist ~ worldly/private ~ giving/receiving.*

*He had never seen such a plethora of personalities presenting from one person: sophisticate/naivete ~ business woman/suburban housewife ~ mother/child ~ enthusiast/ "I don't think so!" bitch ~ client/therapist.*

*They discovered the exquisite
tapestry of characters within,
allowing themselves to shine*

*~*

*consciousness manifest in
human form!*


*There are so many exciting
self-states co-existing in our
human ego-bio suits!*

# Falling in Love
## with
# The Other

After a rendezvous or two,
the lady was ready to move into
romance with the prince.

He was so easy to talk with. He
actually listened when she spoke
and remembered what she said.

Most unusual for the men she
had met up 'til now.

*There was beautiful chemistry between them and the passion was building.*

*Yet the prince guided the couple slowly with gentle affection until the day of consummation arrived.*

*Eight hours of caressing, kissing, and exploring passed by effortlessly and luxuriously ~ leading the new lovers through their first sexual experience together.*

*Then and there the lovely lady
realized the difference between
"having sex" and "making love! "*

*Of course there was also much
playing and laughing
~ extending on and on into
an enchanted evening.*

*It seems the prince's
conscious and compassionate
approach to lovemaking
entwined sensuality
with sexuality.*

*A rich blending of feminine and
masculine energies.*

*Each partner's body, mind, and soul were totally engaged.*

*The lovers effortlessly dropped into a profound state of being ~ experiencing themselves as love itself.*

*It was beginning to feel majical!*

*The hours spent together turned into days, the days into weeks, and the weeks into months*

*~*

*and thus the years flew by!*

*They felt wrapped together
in the lightness of spirit*

*~*

*Tethered by unshakable,
unbreakable bonds of love
and respect.*

*Flowers, candles, soft music,
delicious aromas,  a beautiful
peaceful vibe ~ all welcomed
the lady each time she entered
the prince's home.*

*Ever so gently easing her from
the outside busy/business world
into their private/protective
nest.*

This turned out to be
the perfect setting for an
energetic explosion in the
lovers' lives.

Their sacred sparks
flew fast and furiously ~
igniting a riveting romantic
adventure!

They had come together not
needing anything ~ simply
delighting in the essence
of the other.

*Shortly after their
passionate affair had begun,
the lovely lady hosted a party at
her home.*

*A little while before guests
were to arrive, the prince
noticed the lady was
mega-stressed and offered her
a massage to relax her
mind and body.*

When the prince arrived
to provide the much needed
relaxation ~ he gifted the lady
music he had compiled
and entitled,
"Unconditional Love."

Simultaneously, the charming
prince and the lovely lady
understood this phrase was very
important foreshadowing in
"their story."

For nine and a half weeks,
a sea of passion engulfed them.

Flowing over them, through
them, and like an undertow
delivered them to the depths
of desire, and their destiny.

Their fierce eagerness to serve
the other forced these lovers to
surf the waves of a
giving/receiving tide.

*Ebbing and flowing
like the thrill of breathing!*

# Majical Connection

*After many weeks of bliss and fun, the prince traveled to far away Persia to visit his family ~ and perhaps, become engaged.*

*A year or so before this time in "his story," the handsome prince had met a young woman at a party in his homeland ~ possibly a suitable match for marriage.*

*The prince had been honest
with the lovely lady in
San Ramon ~ a hallmark
of the Persian culture since
ancient times.*

*He had said from day one
that he would prefer to remain
a bachelor.  Only if he met an
appropriate partner would
he marry and have a family.*

*As the lady had already been
married for almost half her life,
and was now divorced ~
she too felt fulfilled with a
fabulous fling!*

While the prince was away
visiting his family, the lady
continued her nightly walks,
and thought about how
in love she felt.

And how confusing it seemed
to contemplate his marriage
to another.

Then one night everything
changed ~ she discovered
the true meaning of
unconditional love.

A thought she had never before
entertained swept through
her mind ~ lighting up every
cell of her body.

"I love him so much that I want
him to be happy ~ even if
that happiness is with
another woman."

The very fiber of her being was
pulsing.

Her heart blew open ~ her entire
body was bursting with love!

*Over time, the intensity of this
incredible feeling faded.*

*But the experience totally
reprogrammed the lady's view
of love forever.*

*Simply thinking about the prince
had produced this gift ~ this
visceral understanding of
profound love.*

*Doesn't the feeling of
loving another come from
somewhere other than the mind?*

*Wasn't being loved more
rewarding than loving?*

*Apparently not!*

During the time of the prince's absence, the lovely lady continued working on her spiritual growth.

Exploring and employing various methods to further expand her mind and heart.

On occasion, the lady would participate in an awakening technique using the breath to access personal and transpersonal insights.

Once, she had a powerful vision
of a tree that grew outside
the prince's abode.

The lovely lady watched,
and then began to feel
the tree bend down and gently
lift her on its branches upwards
into the prince's living room ~
carefully laying her down on his
ivory sofa.

As this unusual awareness
progressed, she became the
color purple and began to
expand and grow.

She grew larger than the
prince's apartment, larger than
San Ramon, larger than the
planet ~ eventually expanding
beyond all she knew of
material form.

The sensation throughout the
experience was that of
pure being ~ pure bliss.

As her consciousness came
back to her familiar reality,
the lovely lady realized that the
insightful journey was foretelling
her further awakening with
the Persian prince.

In less than two months,
the prince  returned to
San Ramon and the lady ~
unengaged & full of many tales.

One of the charming prince's
tales was particularly
compelling.

When the prince had arrived
in Tehran, he was wandering
through a bazaar and was
captivated by two
breathtakingly colorful and
sparkly scarves hanging in
front of one stall.

The prince was drawn to
buy them for the lady, but
as he thought about her rather
conservative taste in clothing,
he decided she would not really
appreciate them.

Meanwhile back in California,
the lady had been taking
belly dancing lessons to surprise
the prince ~ and for fun,
of course.

*Shortly before his return,
the prince called and asked
the lady what she would like
from his country. She answered,
"I would love a scarf to wear
belly dancing!"*

*His stunned silence on the phone
was mistaken by the lady as a
rejection of the idea ~ so she
offered that whatever he would
like to bring her would be
wonderful.*

Immediately, he sped back
to the bazaar, found the stall,
but those scarves were
not hanging there.

The proprietor was otherwise
occupied, and not interested in
helping the prince find these
special gifts.

Then the prince spied
an older vendor he had seen
before at the stall.

This mystical merchant
remembered the handsome
prince and the scarves.

*Before anyone could say,
"true love" the kindly
merchant majically produced
the treasures.*

*The lady swooned at the sight of
the scarves as the prince
bestowed them upon her and
recounted his rousing adventure.*

*Deeper and deeper they fell ~
ecstasy was theirs!*

*When your heart runs your life,
everything works!*

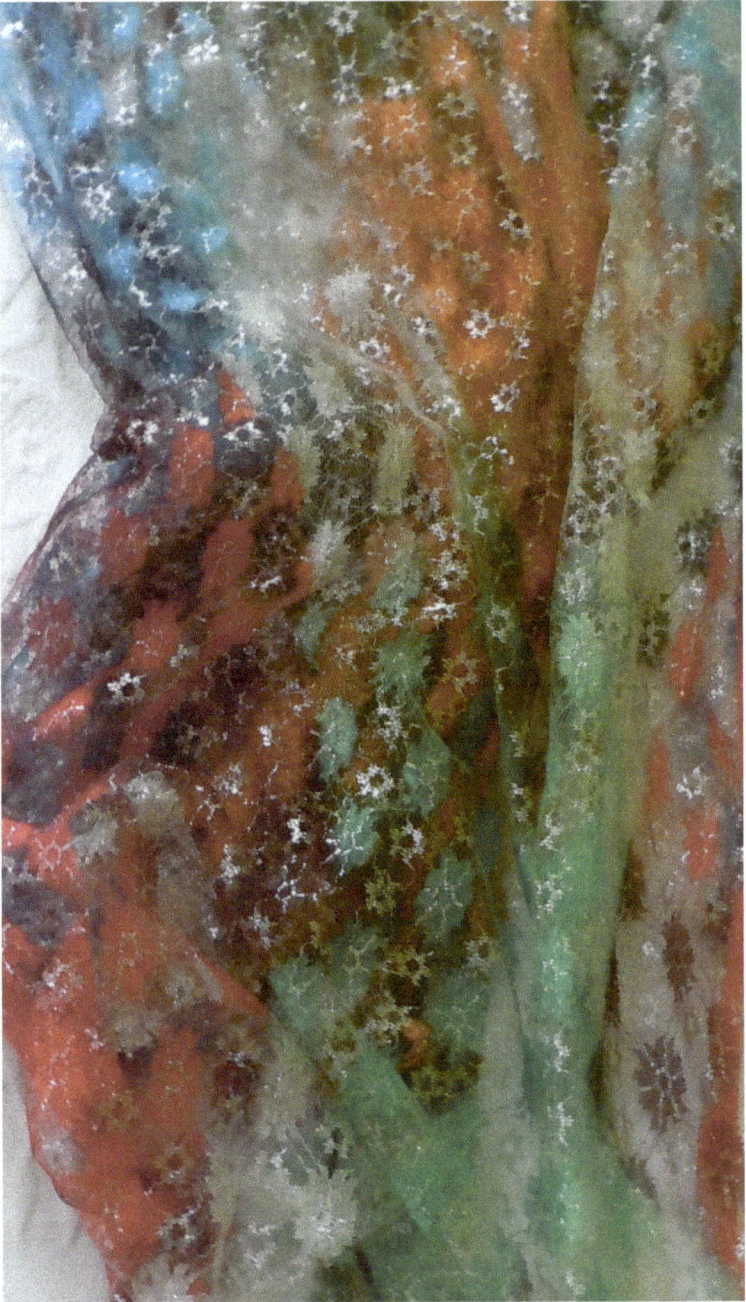

44

# Passion Pain & Play

As the stars aligned to guide
the lovers on their journey,
the Earth revolved and rotated in
amazement that such bliss could
be sustained on its surface.

Alas, the handsome prince and
the lovely lady both sensed that
theirs was not an affair that
would evolve in the traditional
way lovers usually imagine.

The signs could not be denied.

47

One afternoon, at the end of
a rigorous semester in
graduate school, the lady
decided to relax in a delicious
tub bath.

As she closed her eyes and
melted into the water,
an image appeared.

Her prince was standing next to
an exquisite, smiling
woman with dark hair ~
his arm around her in a
warm embrace.

The prince's face radiated love for the woman.  His eyes gently expressed this eventuality.

You can imagine the lovely lady's initial alarm & sad feelings.

She shared her vision with the prince, who consoled the lady with great tenderness.

Before long these difficult feelings gave way to realization and acceptance
~
surely this was foreshadowing of events to come.

*Understanding their time together had a short lifespan, plus the intensity of their passion (like a 10,000 watt bulb) nudged them into periodic separations.*

*Despite their physical distance, the lovers continued to feel a deep connection and awareness of the other ~ like extrasensory perception.*

*Every detachment ~ although usually only a few days ~ was holistically excruciating!*

Once when the lovers separated,
the lady was in such emotional
agony that it felt as if her body
would disintegrate from the
pain.

Her beautiful daughter
suggested the lonely lady sit in
a closet, letting the clothes
hang down around her
in the dark.

The womb effect worked well!

*With her daughter's help,
the lovely lady began to
reintegrate the pieces of
her being.*

*Processing her ego's caricature
over and over ~ looking less like
her former self every day.*

*As for the prince ~ occupying
himself with his painting, and
reading books on spiritual
wisdom sustained him through
these painful breakup periods.*

*Both lovers busy growing
and maturing on their paths!*

*Each partner learning to
navigate the reprogramming
of all ideas regarding
love versus attachment.*

*Thus, they advanced and
stumbled toward wholeness.*

*Vacillating between the
self-state that believed loss
is undesirable ~ or even possible
~ and the Self within that IS
unconditional love.*

When the lovers were together
they lit up the universe.

It felt as if they were making love
for the whole world.

Those who witnessed them
together remarked how unusual
it was to find such a majical love.

These two people showering
each other with positive energy
produced an atmosphere of joy
for everyone around!

*On warm sunny afternoons
the lovers languished outside
the prince's petite palace.*

*It was their pleasure to drink in
source energy from the sun,
run it through their hearts and
bodies ~ basking in the bliss of
divine love!*

In their love cocoon, the lovely
lady discovered and embraced
her exotic & erotic sides.

The prince's collection of sensual
Middle Eastern music evoked
divine feminine energy from
deep within her.

Her ancient soul corded to
the depths of Mother Earth.

The lovely lady could dance
for hours ~ weaving the cultures
through time and space ~
recognizing and revealing their
common denominator ~ LOVE.

On warm full moon evenings
the lovers basked and beamed
in the celestial rays.

It always felt as if even more
love and light were being
switched on inside of them.

And yet they made no promises
to each other.

After all, promises seem simply
feeble attempts to predict
the future.

Free to be in the moment,
unencumbered, is truly precious.

*Regularly, our romantic couple discussed a broad range of subjects.*

*And of course, their favorite topic was love.*

*One question they explored was, "Is it possible to be in love with two people at the same time?"*

As the true nature of love
shifted old programming in
their psyches, the answer arose:

The feeling of "being in love"
is our natural state!

The lovers realized that only
their beliefs and fears had kept
them from this knowledge.

When we are aware of this
indwelling love, no "other" is
necessary.

Nice, to be sure!
But not necessary to feel love.

After some time of the lovely lady telling the handsome prince how beautiful he was, the prince inquired,

"Aren't women usually thought of as beautiful, and men called handsome?"

"That's true," she replied, "but I see so much love shining through you ~ you're full of beauty!"

"If you weren't a person, what
would you like to be?"
the prince asked.

"A palm tree," the lady said.
"They're graceful, offer
protection and fruit, and grow in
warm climates.  And you?"

The prince answered he would
like to be a rock ~
solid and supportive.

And so they were.

*One Valentine's Day, the lady arrived at her apartment and found her bedroom door closed.*

*A spectacular sight lay before her as she entered her boudoir ~ M&Ms of all colors were strewn everywhere!*

*Of course, there was a
hand painted card and
box of chocolates propped on
the pillows ~ but the deep sense
of fun and excitement that those
hundreds of colored dots around
the room evoked could not be
matched.*

*Keep your child-state alive and
healthy, allowing it expression as
often as possible!*

# Cultural Filters

*As the couple revealed them selves to each other, their early ego conditioning came to light.*

*The charming prince had grown up in a privileged family in the Middle East.*

*He often spoke about how loving his parents were. Their boundless generosity toward everyone.*

*For instance, when the prince
was a child, his mother would
take him to visit a psychiatric
hospital ~ bringing patients
treats and kind words to
brighten their day.*

*The prince was greatly
impacted by these visits ~
realizing how fortunate he was,
and how small thoughtful acts
can make such a difference
in the world.*

Like we all do, the handsome prince had plans for how his life would unfold.

He would travel to far off America to earn a degree in engineering and become proficient in English.

This part of his plan came to fruition.

However, his goal of returning to the beautiful, peaceful Iran he remembered was not available to him when his education was complete.

*A deep grief welled up within
the prince's heart and psyche.*

*Among fleeting feelings of
sadness and sorrow,
he painted, continued
reprogramming himself, and
accepted this change in
his projected storyline.*

*And so the prince graduated
with his engineering degree,
began his career, and made his
home in California.*

As for the lovely lady, she
was born on the other side
of the world ~ growing up on a
dairy farm in the United States.

The lady's parents had also been
raised in privileged families ~
with a great emphasis on
etiquette.

Later in life, as the lady evolved,
she realized that formality is
actually designed to disguise
discomfort.

A framework of rules helps
one mask vulnerability.

And so, hippies at heart
before it was fashionable,
the lady's parents traded the
comfort of their upbringing to
"live close to the land,"
as people said in
those days.

Every day was rich in
plants, animals, flowers and soil
~
a cornucopia of delights for
any child!

*Following high school, the lovely lady left for France to study at the Universite Paris - Sorbonne.*

*In France she discovered many interesting customs and ideas that challenged her beliefs about the "American Dream."*

*The lady's travels throughout Europe continued to open her mind and heart to the myriad possibilities for living out "our stories."*

*Once the lady returned to North America, a strong desire to marry and have children ~ programmed by her mother and society ~ led the lady back into her familiar culture.*

*Thus the lovely lady's early adult years were spent fulfilling the proscribed protocol for American women at that time.*

*Fortunately, her marriage and children were exciting and satisfying events in the lovely lady's life.*

*Now an interesting evolution arose out of our lovers' union.*

*The prince and the lady had come from entirely different cultures ~ many of their beliefs differed irreconcilably.*

*Miraculously, they allowed the differences to be just as they were.*

*Each saw life through carefully programmed cultural filters.*

Yet under the fire of great passion, the need to be right gave way to tolerance and acceptance.

Unconditional love flourished ~ despite the occasional moments spent mired in the manure of thinking.

That may sound like strong phraseology.

However, as many have come to understand, thinking is one of western society's most prevalent addictions.

*Thinking (especially critiquing)*
*is perhaps the most*
*painful dependency for*
*everyone involved!*

*Information codifies our reality.*

*The less we have defined*
*anything or everything ~*
*the less limitations*
*we have built on an experience ~*
*the more majic & miracles have*
*permission to appear.*

*The prince and the lady thought as little as possible.*

*This strategy allowed them to stay present and keep their hearts open ~ imperative for unconditional loving!*

*Dualistic friction disappeared ~ no right/wrong ~ good/bad ~ high/low ~ here/there ~ only blinding love for each other and everyone & everything around them.*

One night the lady was outdoors
awaiting the prince's arrival
for her beautiful daughter's
graduation from a school of
healing arts.

As the lady watched
the handsome prince approach,
the earth moved beneath her feet
~ she drifted down and floated
up all at the same time...

swallowed up whole by love!

These moments are beyond
fabricated projections ~ what we
usually mistake for love ~
no thought, only presence and
feeling.

To get these glimpses of "heaven"
we have only to be.

*When thinking stops, time seems
to stop. We can feel the peace of
pure consciousness.*

# Embracing Wholeness

Often, when the Persian prince
spoke, the lovers could hear
the sound of ancient times in
the timber of his voice ~ a vocal
vining of past and present
energies.

According to the prince, no one
had ever before mentioned
this eerie quality in his speech.

Yet he knew his soul
was somehow connected to the
antiquity of his culture.

*Reading poetry of Hafiz ~
a 14th century enlightened
Persian poet ~ had become the
prince's favorite past time.*

*He would chant just one line,
study the commentary
explaining its essence, and then
assimilate what Hafiz had
discovered about the
mystery of life.*

*Another effective method of
reprogramming!*

*Much of the wisdom*
*the charming prince shared*
*with the lovely lady came from*
*these teachings.*

*Just as the lady's talented son*
*was able to recite Shakespeare's*
*writing so that the old English*
*languaging could be easily*
*understood*

*~*

*So the prince, in his chanting of*
*Hafiz' verses, was able to embody*
*and convey the wise poet's*
*intended message.*

To begin an offering of spiritual insight, the charming prince would often say, "The thing is..." and then break off to laugh and ask with his endearing Persian accent, "Should I tell you the thing?"

And the lovely lady always responded with eagerness and humor, "Yes, tell me the thing!"

*Through coincidences and synchronicities, the lovers wove their lives on and on.*

*Albeit a bit befuddled by their intense attraction ~ after all this wasn't going to last, the passionate couple continued laughing, learning, and loving.*

*From time to time, the charming prince would remark about the love they shared ~ so profound and unusual.*

He would say, "So few ever experience what we have together ~ there must be a reason this is happening to us."

At first, when the prince would refer to their relationship as an experience, the lovely lady recoiled ~ feeling this expression denigrated their amazing connection.

Eventually she came to see that everything in life is just that ~ an experience to be appreciated.

*It appeared these lovers'
souls were woven together
through lifetimes.*

*Sometimes memories emerged of
having been in other roles
together with other backdrops in
"other stories."*

*Each lifetime when they meet
they know they will not be able
to stay together ~ yet they do not
want to know this.*

*The exquisite agony of
beginnings and endings!*

In this lifetime, the prince
encouraged the lady to spend
time alone, to paint, to cook,
to feel deeply ~ all for her own
pleasure.

Once when the lady had a cold
and wasn't feeling so well,
the prince reminded her to savor
the experience.

"Enjoy life like a fine meal ~
appreciate all its aspects,"
he would say.

Sometimes an event would arise
that the lady did not enjoy.

The prince always encouraged
her to step courageously into
the uncomfortable areas in life.

"Don't miss out!" he cautioned.

The prince also chided her to not
be a slave to her things.

"Who is this guy?" she wondered
~ she had never looked at life
this way!

*The lady showed the prince how to keep committed relationships fun ~ with partners, family and friends ~ of which she seemed to have gazillions!*

*She modeled parenting ~ truly enjoying her adult children ~ allowing them to teach her more than she needed to teach them.*

*And most importantly, during their time together, the prince learned that happiness is a choice.*

*We never really teach anyone anything ~ everything is already inside of us ~ we remember when we're ready.*

*Romantic relationship is designed to provide a safe environment in which remembering is facilitated.*

*We are able to rediscover our selves in the other.*

*This is not to say one needs to enter a romantic relationship to learn to love oneself ~ there are many ways to do that.*

*This is to say unconditional self-love is the primary benefit for the ego once one enters into romance.*

*Many wise folk have said ~ relationships are assignments to help us learn who we are.*

*So many wonderful things happened when these lovers stepped out of their comfort zones ~ met each other and themselves in new, unchartered territory.*

*It was breathtaking to
watch their surrender
to the rawness of the Tao,
with fear and trust interwoven
~ souls ripped open and re-sewn
into the feeling of oneness at the
edge of duality.*

*Known by awakening seekers as
"the razor's edge!"*

*As passionate as making love
was for this couple ~ what was
really electrifying was their
energetic exchange.*

*This effusion of love was a
palpable expression of their
majic together.*

*An intoxicating outpouring ~
an epicurean feast for all
around them.*

*Friends and family said they
experienced the effects of
electric energy between the
prince & the lady ~ such that
the vibrations felt good in their
own bodies ~ pulling them into
the lovers' vast vortex.*

The lady's son-in-law once
described the lovers' sensual
approach to most interactions
with material form, "They dine
while others eat."

*Dining is with grace & appreciation.*
*Eating is with gusto & satiation!*

Open and vulnerable in
a chrysalis of love, the lady and
the prince were able to explore,
express, and embrace all
self-states, including
their shadow sides

~

freedom!

*They discovered that wholeness
is the ultimate beauty shining
through each being.*

*We all need to be witnessed with
love and compassion until
we can do it for ourselves.*

*Sometimes our parents do this
for us early on ~ sometimes it
occurs later in life's story.*

*Now our lovers were open to
reprogramming themselves
~ seeking out opportunities
to do so.*

*For instance, the handsome*
*prince got the lovely lady to*
*SIT DOWN.*

*This was quite a feat*
*~ especially given that*
*she was a product of the 1950s,*
*who believed she was*
*obliged to wait hand and foot on*
*everyone on Earth,*
*who was an Enneagram*
*"Enthusiast," and*
*who had a Gemini sun with*
*double Sagittarius moon*
*and ascendant.*

*This lady never sat down ~
except to drive 1-2 hours in any
direction for a meal or visit with
one of her gazillion friends.*

*A gazillion friends!  That's not
normal ~ must be a phobia,
probably abandonment ~ or
a defense mechanism, maybe
defending against feeling lonely
~ or an addiction,
possibly a gluttony of friends.*

*OR... perhaps it's simply the programming for our lovely lady at this point in "her story," which leads ~ as we know now, here in the future ~ to all the other wonderful parts of her life.*

*It's all how we choose to look at it!*

*In sharp contrast to the lovely lady's hummingbird-style programming, the charming prince was born under a Libra sun, and was an Enneagram "Peacemaker."*

*Thus, the prince most often
appeared patient, calm,
and easy-going.*

*As the wise prince watched
the lovely lady expending
energy for family and her
gazillion friends,
he encouraged her to attend to
her own needs first.*

*Reminding her to remain
strong & flexible ~
maintaining balance in her
body and psyche.*

*One way the lady would
call forth pain for herself was
to get tangled in ideas
about the future.*

*In answer to the lady's requests
regarding future activities,
the wise prince would often say,
"Let's wait and see."*

*Now this was also a phrase
the lady's father had used when
she was a young girl ~
so you can guess that those
words triggered past
frustration and disappointment.*

*The lady was a heavy-duty planner by nature.*

*However, with coaching from the patient prince, the light dawned for the lovely lady.*

*She realized she actually preferred arriving in the future without planned commitments*

*~*

*freedom!*

*Wonderful things happen when we face our fears and step out of our comfort zones!*

# The Year
## of
# Everything

The lady's astrological configuration ~ described before ~ indicated it was imperative for her to travel rather extensively.

So about three years into their relationship she left for a three month excursion to India ~ an inner and outer exploration.

On her journey, she was
introduced to silent meditation,
a slower paced culture, and a
new lens through which
to view life.

After a week in this wildly
interesting country, a young
woman asked the lady how
she was enjoying India.

The lady replied by listing the
difficulties she had faced so far.

With great wisdom the woman
said, "If you're not enjoying
India, you're going too fast."

It's so true for the speed at which
we move through life as well!

Throughout the lovely lady's tour
of India, phone conversations
with the charming prince
encouraged her along the path
of self-discovery.

"I can do this, I can do this,"
the lady would chant to get her
through tough times in India.

It's a mantra that works
wonders in difficult situations
anywhere!

*Meanwhile, back in California ~
while awaiting the lady's return
~ the prince faced the death of
a close friend.*

*The night his friend left, he
visited the prince in spirit ~ they
had a warm, loving exchange.*

*The prince did not realize then
that this was the last time
they would meet in
"this story."*

*Despite his deep grief, the prince did not share this news with his traveling lady.*

*He was concerned she would abort her journey and return to his side.*

*Only once the lady was home and rested, did the prince share the devastating news.*

*Together they grieved, and remembered their friend fondly.*

During their three-month hiatus,
the lady and the prince had
each matured personally.

The challenges & obstacles they
faced revealed the profound
inner strength and resources
that had developed
while immersed in their
unconditional love.

After months apart,
the lovers celebrated their
reunion ~ reveling in their
growth, and rekindling their
intense passion!

*Always ~ at least it seemed
that way ~ when the lovely lady
needed some sage advice,
the Persian prince was there
with words of wisdom.*

*One evening, the lady was
thinking about her dad dying
and a few other
impending losses.*

*As she watched the sun
disappear below the horizon,
anxiety about even its departure
overwhelmed her.*

*She called the wise prince
immediately and relayed her
dismay at losing the sun.*

*He sweetly reminded the
sad lady that people were
waiting for sunlight on the
other side of the earth ~
and of course it would return
tomorrow for her pleasure.*

*And then the year of
EVERYTHING arrived!*

*While she was working long
hours at two internships ~
the lady's father died ~
her beautiful daughter had a
spiritual emergence ~
she helped plan and carry off her
beautiful daughter's wedding ~
and this was the last year of
romance for our lovers.*

*Throughout the "year of
everything," the charming prince
continued cherishing and
supporting the lady.*

*Always providing words of wisdom, preparing delicious, nourishing meals, and maintaining a safe haven for daily restoration.*

*The lovely lady loved watching the prince move about the kitchen as he prepared their food.*

*His movements were like a dancer on a stage ~ the performance and culinary results were art forms!*

*She felt fed in so many ways.*

During that very year, the
lovely lady was granted an
amazing experience.

The morning of her
51st birthday, she awoke early,
crept into the living room
to keep from disturbing
the prince, and began dancing to
some of her favorite music.

The night before, the prince had
offered that they do whatever
the lady desired for the whole of
her birthday.

So naturally, the happy,
pampered lady was wondering,
"How good can I stand it today?"

As she danced that morning,
a small voice in her head
suggested she line up her
chakras.

Chakras are said to be the
energy vortices within our body
along and parallel to the
vertebrae ~ connecting us
to both spiritual and
material realms.

She had never thought of doing this before, but it seemed compelling.

With some concentration she visualized her chakras, set them spinning with energy, and guided them into a straight line from the base of her spine to the crown of her head.

The moment she realized the chakras were aligned her whole body began moving forward and back like a wave.

Then her body began
throbbing ~ culminating in a
profound full body orgasm!

The lady could not move ~
she was "blissed out."

After a long time of immobility,
probably two or three minutes,
she was able to shuffle her feet
toward the bedroom where
the prince lay sleeping.

*The lovely lady was still buzzing as she sat on the bed and announced that she was in a full body orgasm.*

*The prince flashed his beautiful smile, "That's wonderful ~ Happy Birthday!"*

*If romance is taken lightly and with much humor, the journey is extremely pleasurable!*

# Falling in Love
## with
# The Self

Well, this is the part of the
story where the handsome prince
and the lovely lady end the
romantic aspect of their
relationship.

The prince knew it was time to
experience marriage
and family life.

He had the good fortune to meet
a fabulous young woman ~
a doctor to boot!

Lo and behold, this was the very
woman who had appeared
beside the prince in the
lovely lady's vision,
several years before.

During this time of transition,
the prince processed his
feelings through art.

*Passionately painting palm trees, chanting Hafiz, renovating a home for the next chapter of his life story, and stepping fully into his artist role.*

*Shortly after the lovers' shift in relationship, the lovely lady's beautiful daughter happened upon the prince.*

*As they hugged and chatted, she noticed he was actually looking through her eyes ~ as if he were searching for the essence of the lady there.*

*Suddenly sensing the depth
of his passion, the daughter got
a glimpse into the intensity of
the lovers' private world.*

*And in that moment,
she better understood the agony
she had watched her mother
traverse during
each separation.*

~

*As for the lady, well she moved to
Brasil to help found
a healing retreat, and for some
more life-changing experiences.*

Not that it was easy to make
the transition.  The lady
experienced panic at first.

It seemed there was not enough
air to breathe, enough water
to quench her thirst, or enough
food to satisfy her hunger.

Excrutiating emotions signaling
approaching death for
the ego-bio suit.

She too began to paint to pacify
the pain of losing the prince.

Sharing their artwork years
later, the lovers noticed they
each had painted two flowers
standing together ~ one a bit
taller than the other.

Those who know the lovers,
say their extra-sensory
perception is still keen today ~
always connected through
the ethers.

At the end of their era of
romance, the handsome prince
felt bad ~ the lovely lady
felt bad about herself.

She felt she had lost the prize.

As she progressed on her
spiritual path, she realized,
"I am the prize!"

Her time with the prince was
only to wake her up to
that truth.

*While in his care, she had felt like the most cherished prize.*

*Now it was time for her to practice cherishing her self*

*~*

*freedom!*

Our lovers had seen their
reflections in the eyes of
the beloved other ~ and that
reflection told them how
lovable they were.

The beautiful part of this
scenario is that as
we look out at "the other"
~ we are always seeing a
reflection of ourselves.

From that vantage point,
we can fall in love with
who we truly are.

*In fact, the lovely lady always felt she appeared the most ravishing whenever she looked into the mirror at the prince's home.*

*She was able to see herself through her lover's eyes.*

## *Romantic Love is Falling in Love with Yourself*

And if we can remember this going into relationship, we will always leave more whole than when we began.

What we are currently experiencing in our human evolution is that romance often begins with euphoria and ends with agony.

Such a painful pattern for the players!

*As with all patterns, of course, our ability to see what's happening between euphoria and agony determines our ability to dance with it.*

*Keeping our hearts open to all the parts of our selves ~ and our partners ~ often leads us to unconditional love.*

*This could be the end of romantic tragedy!*

Like all emotions, feelings of loss are a normal part of life, and can be savored.

And ultimately we can reframe changes in our relationships, careers, environments, or even stages of our lives as graduation!

Always moving into and through the next part of "the story."

*When we stay loosely attached to
the plot, it's easier to stay
in the Tao ~ the flow of life.*

*Now during the lovers'
time together, the lady's
physical form had begun its
changes ~ in the way women's
bodies have been programmed to
morph and prepare for the
next chapter of their lives.*

*As the prince was nearly a
decade younger than the lady,
he had not been with anyone
going through this event.*

*The lovely lady was a bit hesitant
to discuss her new status ~ she
wondered if their age difference
would seem all the more.*

*However, in his usual way,
the charming prince offered
with warmth and enthusiasm,
"Congratulations ~
you've become a woman!"*

*The prince had learned,
and was now gently offering,
to focus on the wine
rather than the glass.*

And so the lovely lady became
a wonderful woman.

Indeed she was full of wonder at
the richness of her life.

The wonderful woman finally felt
like the peach her Persian prince
had perceived when they first
met many years before.

Once we have ripened, we taste
better ~ to ourselves
and to others!

*Fortunately, our lovers learned
this secret:*

*The way to freedom is to love
our selves as we love the other.*

*Creating balance between
the inside and the outside
of the self
~
majical love!*

The truly majical part of this
story is that the Persian prince
and the lovely lady ~ now
a wonderful woman ~ stayed in
unconditional love
with each other ~ & everyone ~
& everything.

But those are other tales
for another day.

*~ And they lived happily ever after ~*

*The Beginning*

144

# Offerings

We love ourselves by saying
loving things to our selves ~
listening to our selves ~ giving
the body nurturing and affection
~ loving our selves as we love
others.

It heals our pain, like majic!

Can we love ourselves all

the time?

~

no matter what!

The key is to learn to love
everything about ourselves.

~

Then we have the Creator's
perspective.

We are the cake

in our lives

~

all else is frosting.

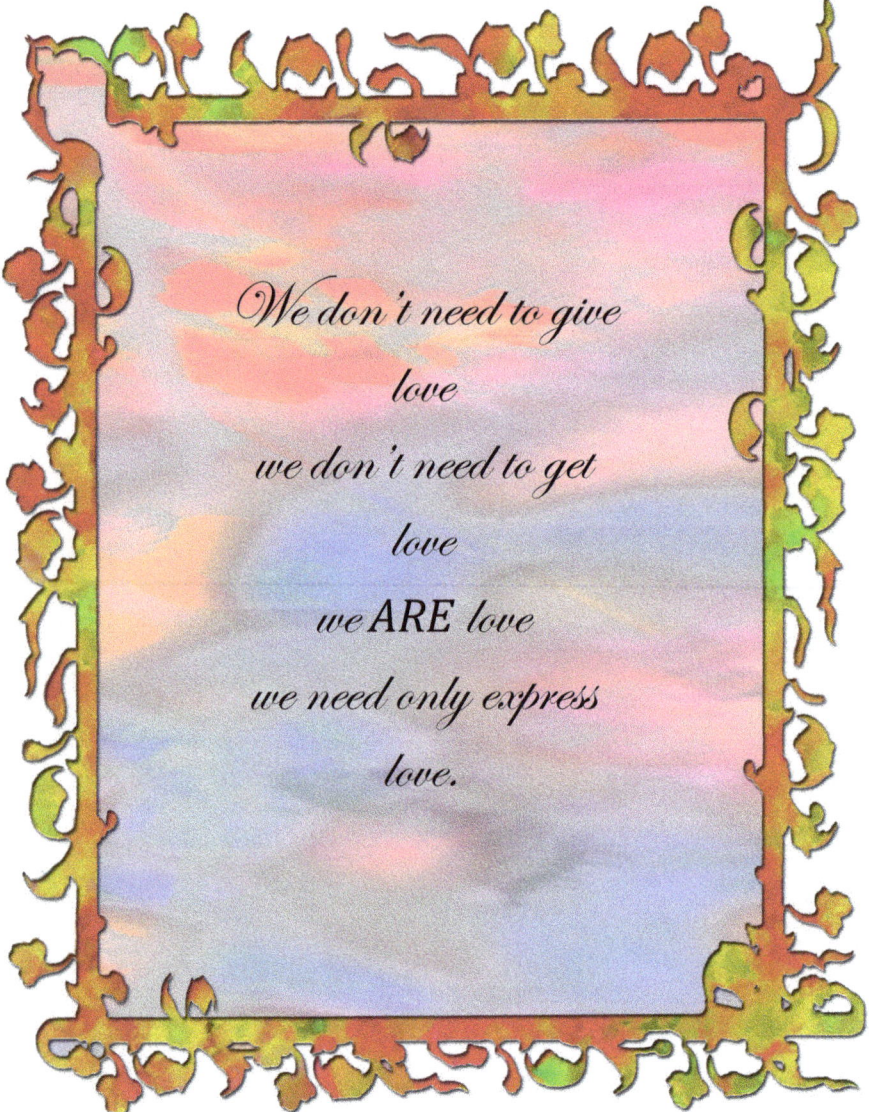

We don't need to give

love

we don't need to get

love

we ARE love

we need only express

love.

*Romance is a game
we made up to feel good,
and feel bad, and
experience the human story
deeply.*

In the story of Narcissus,
the fellow consumed with his
own beauty falls into the water
and drowns.
In romantic relationships,
often the lovers drown in
the beauty of the other ~
not realizing it is simply
their own reflection.

153

The goal is to live fully

~

alone ~ with one partner

a few ~ or more!

*Above all, we're here to love
each other as our selves
unconditionally.*

*Above all, to see the beauty,
treasures, and talents within
each of life's creations.*

*Above all, to stare until we see
the light in everything.*

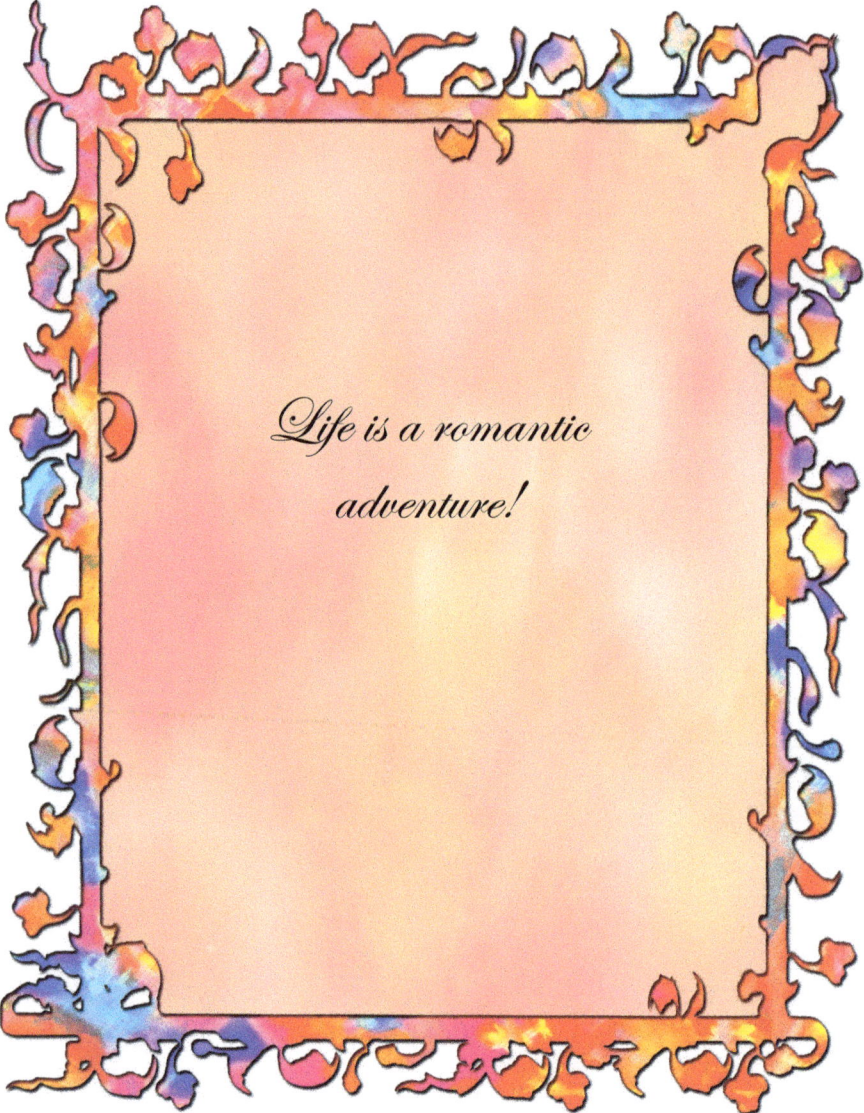

*Life is a romantic*

*adventure!*

*May these offerings tug at your heart,*
*your mind, and your soul.*


*With love from,*
*Behnam & Gaia*

# Acknowledgments

*It is with great gratitude and
an avalanche of appreciation that
we acknowledge those people whose
presence and support contributed to
our story ~ allowing it to unfold
and be told.*

*Naturally, we are immensely
grateful for this incarnation,
giving first thanks to our parents ~
Shirley & Robert, and Forough & Ali.*

*Our abiding love and appreciation go
out to Behnam's wife, Sepideh, who ~
with their children, Kiyan & Darya ~
lovingly sustained us through the
creation of this offering.*

*Bountiful blessings to Francine,
the catalyst and patient participant
in this love affair/awakening.*

*And David, a true renaissance man,
enriched our lives with his merriment
and evolved perspectives.*

*Our sisters, Behrokh and Sallie, also
entered into the romance ~ along
with a gazillion friends and relatives
~ Bahman, Bahram, Leela, George,
Michael, Rhonda, Reza, and Rebecca
~ just to name a precious few.*

*Thank you ~ Merci!*

# About The Artist

*Behnam Nouri, B.S.*
*is a painter, and graphic designer.*

*He has a Bachelor of Science Degree*
*in Engineering from California State*
*University,  Los Angeles, CA.*

# About The Author

*Gaia Waxman, Psy.D.,*
*is an awakening psychotherapist*
*and reprogramming facilitator.*

*With fun and sensitivity,*
*she promotes cultivation of*
*unconditional love ~ personally,*
*interpersonally, and transpersonally.*

*Gaia holds a doctorate in*
*Clinical Psychology from California*
*Institute of Integral Studies,*
*San Francisco, CA.*

www.gaia-awakening.com

Look in the mirror

And you will be in love too

Rumi